ALPHABET
LEARNING
BOOK

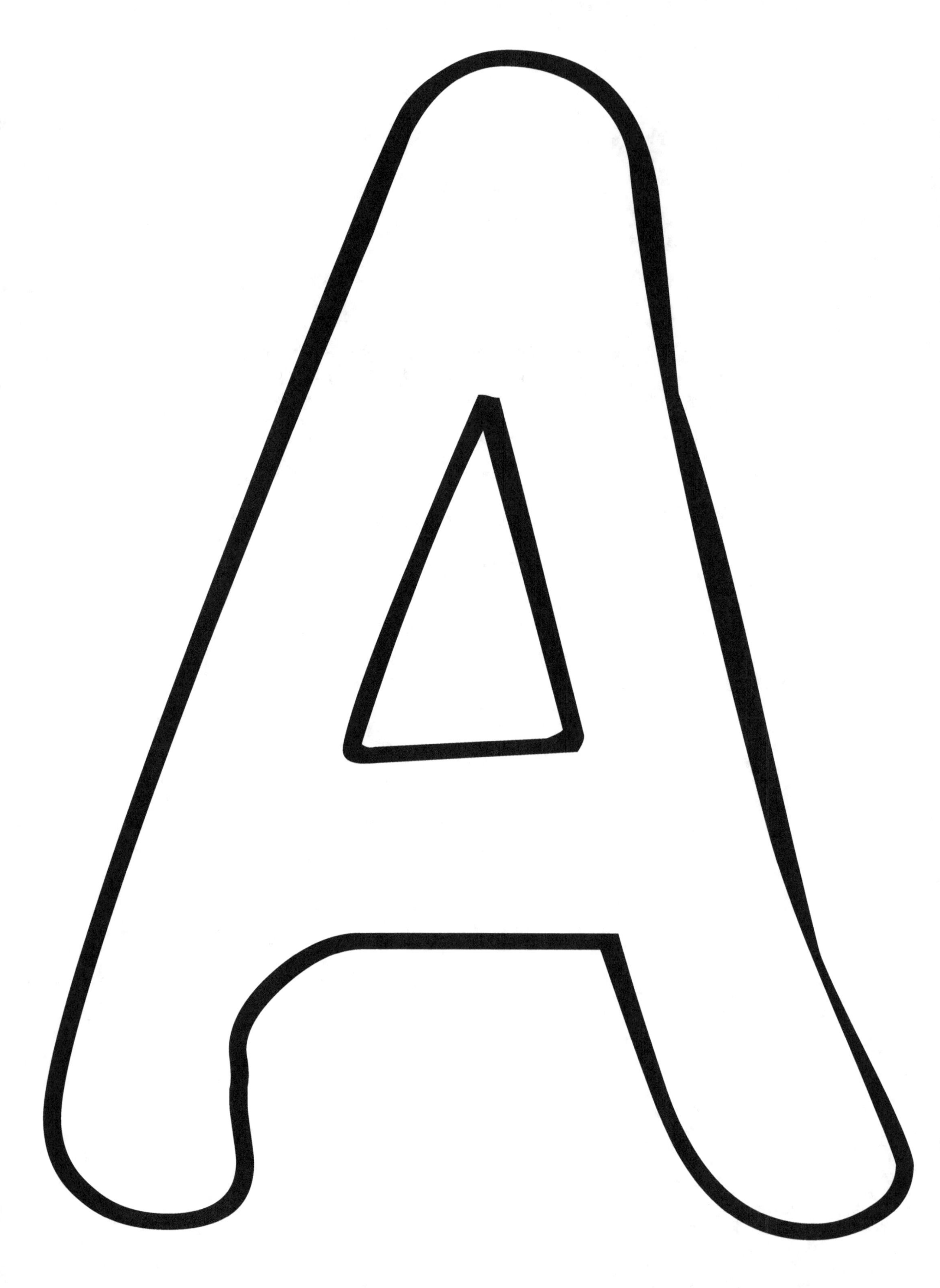

A a is for
Apple

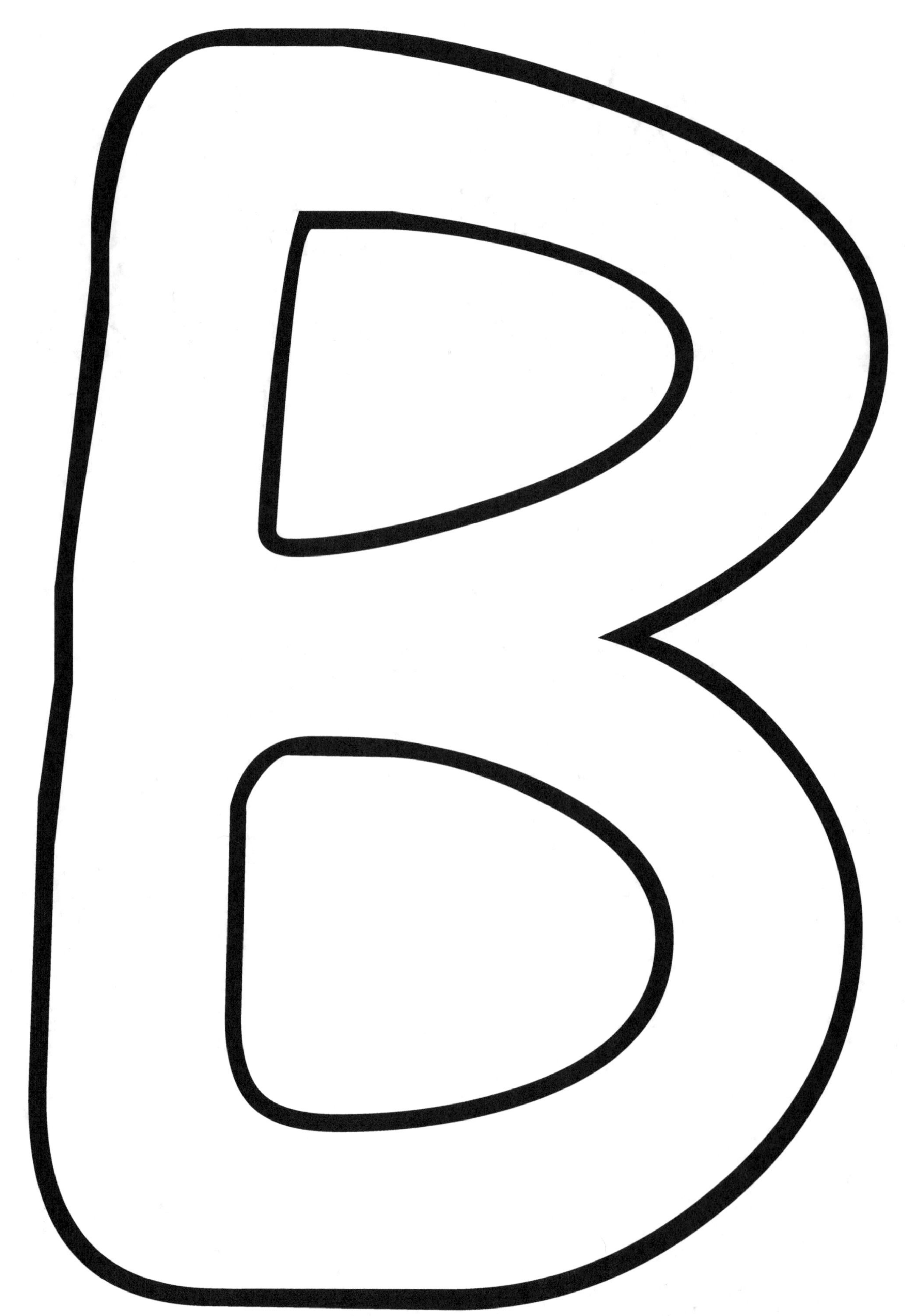

Bb
is for
BOW

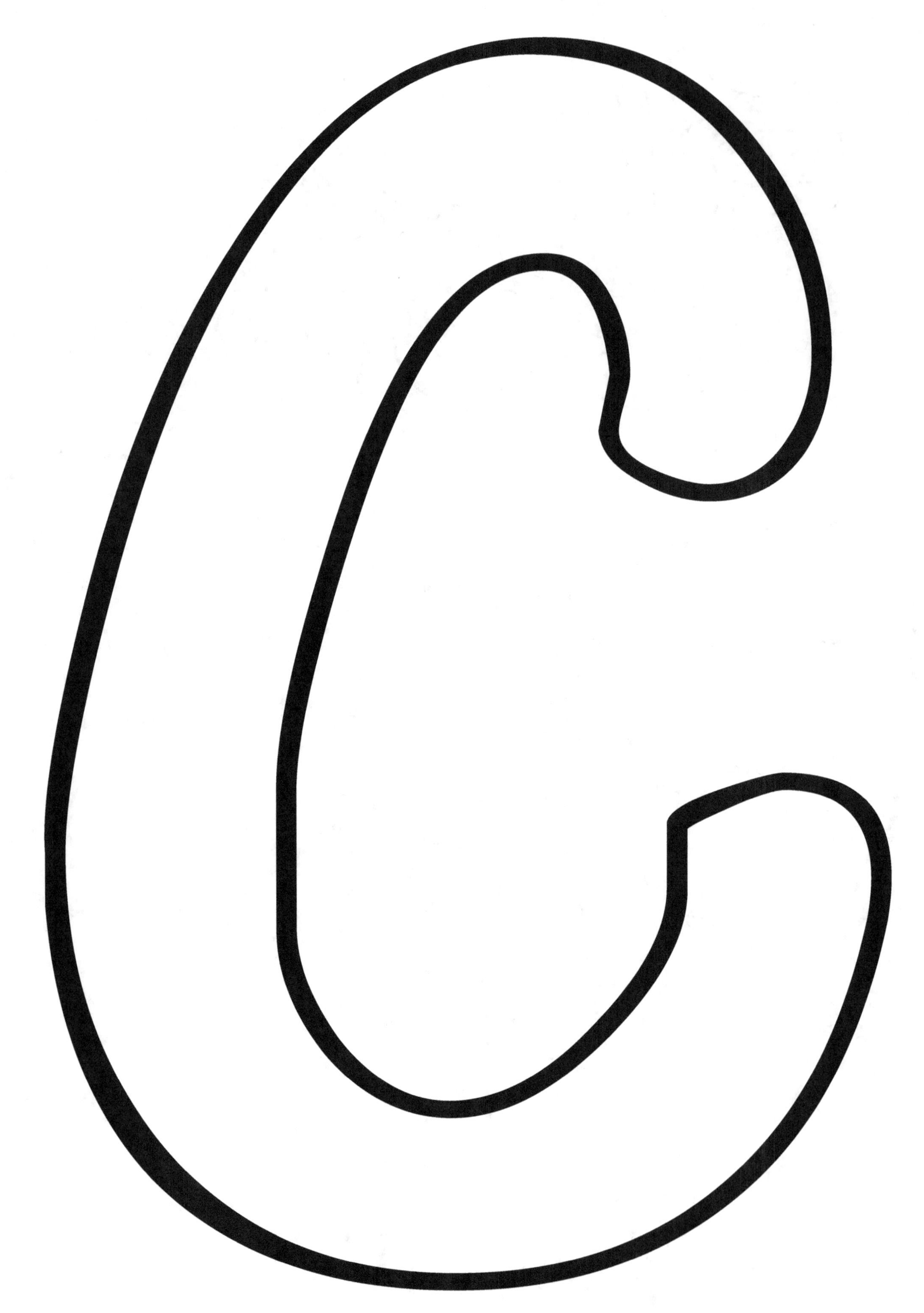

Cc
is for
Cock

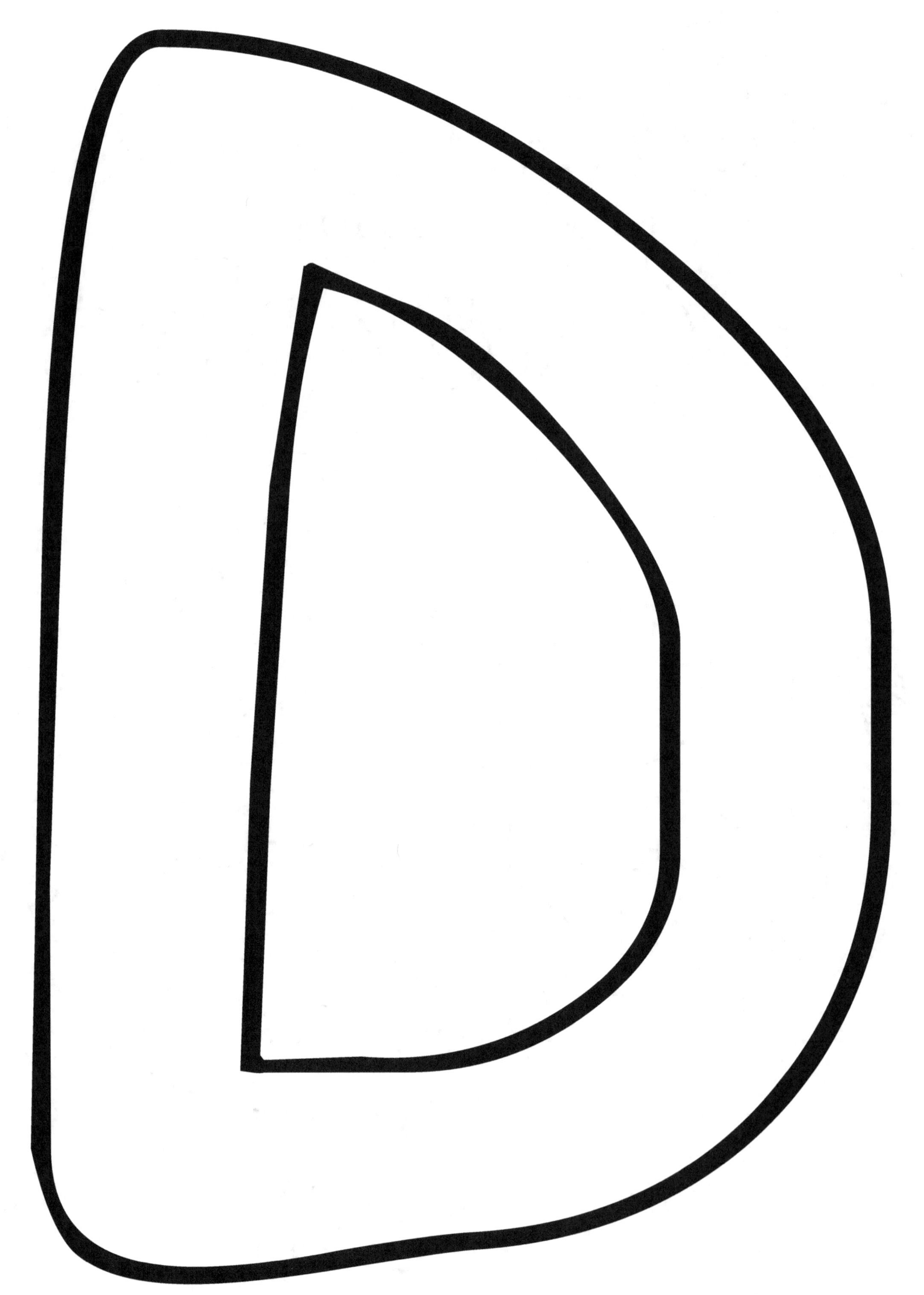

Dd is for
Dog

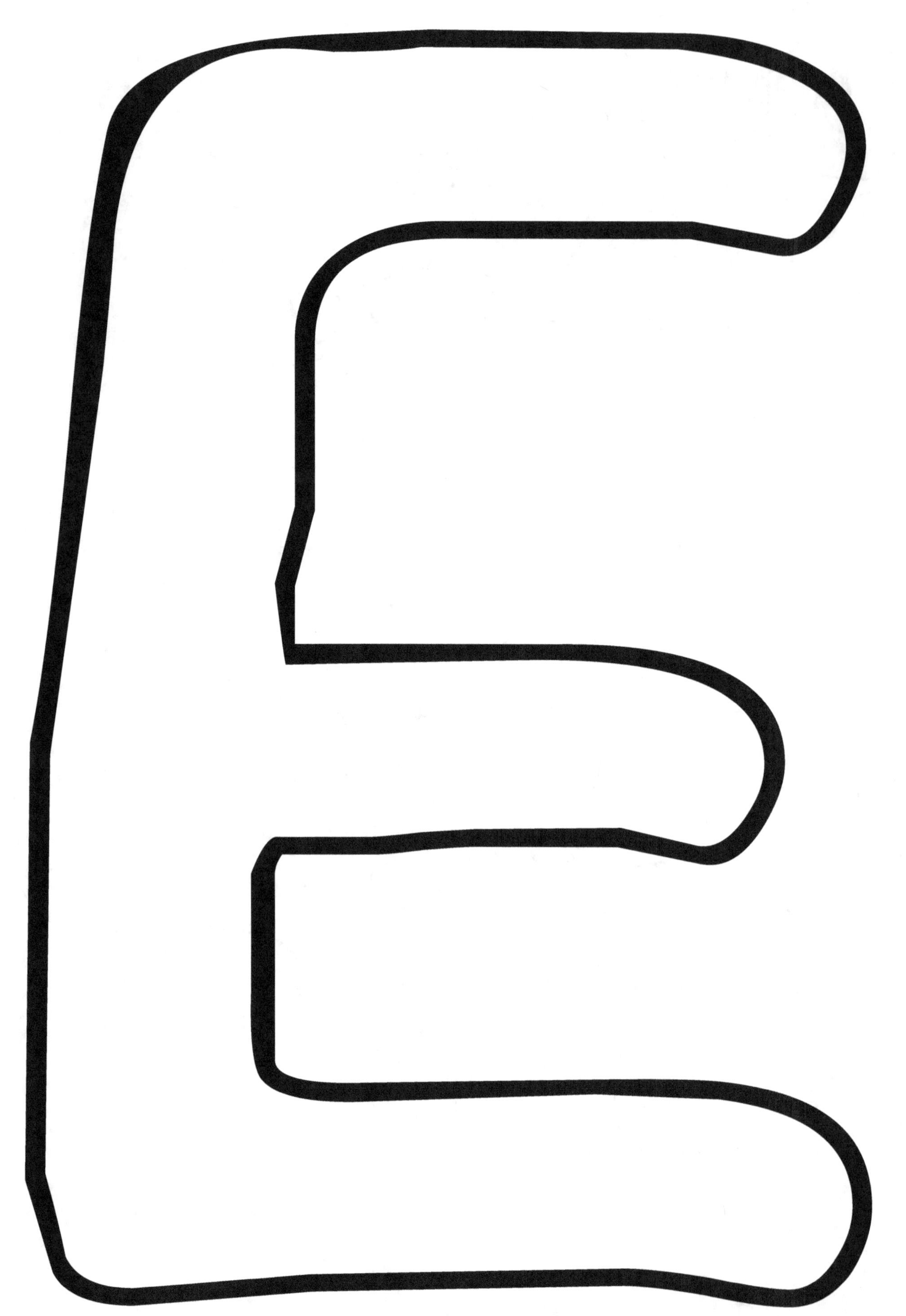

Ee is for Elephant

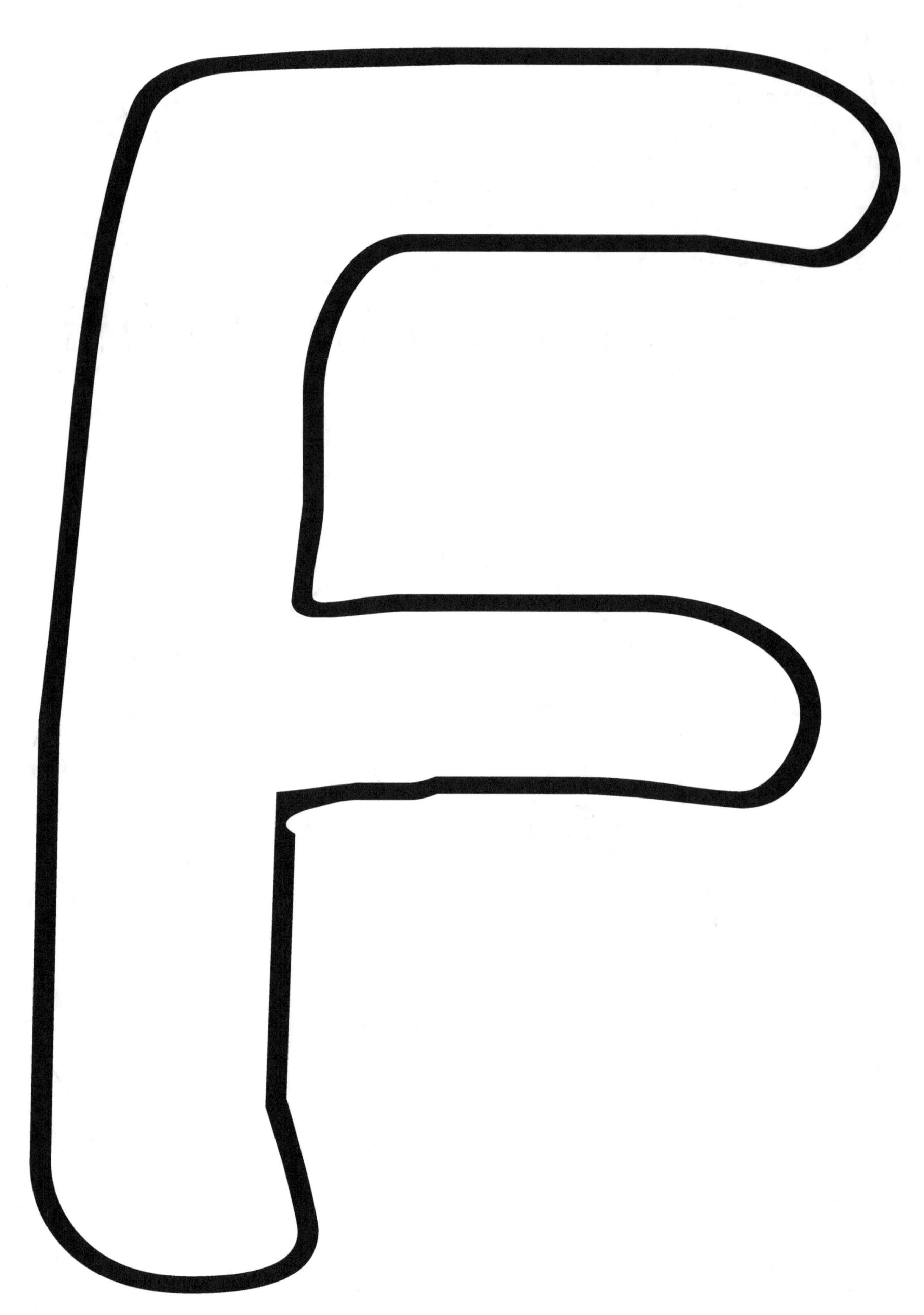

F f is for

Fish

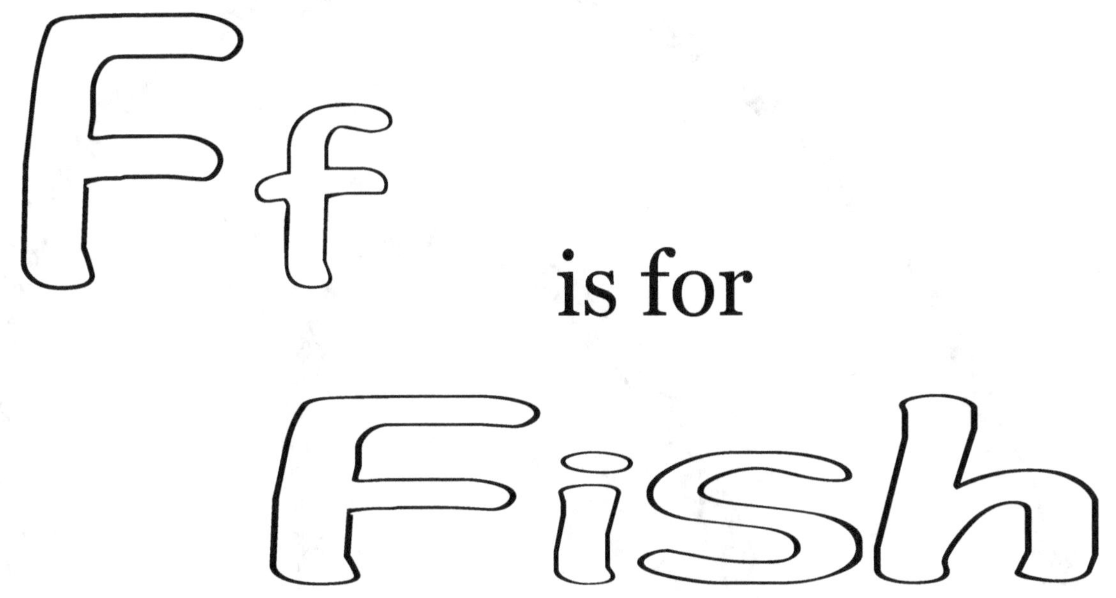

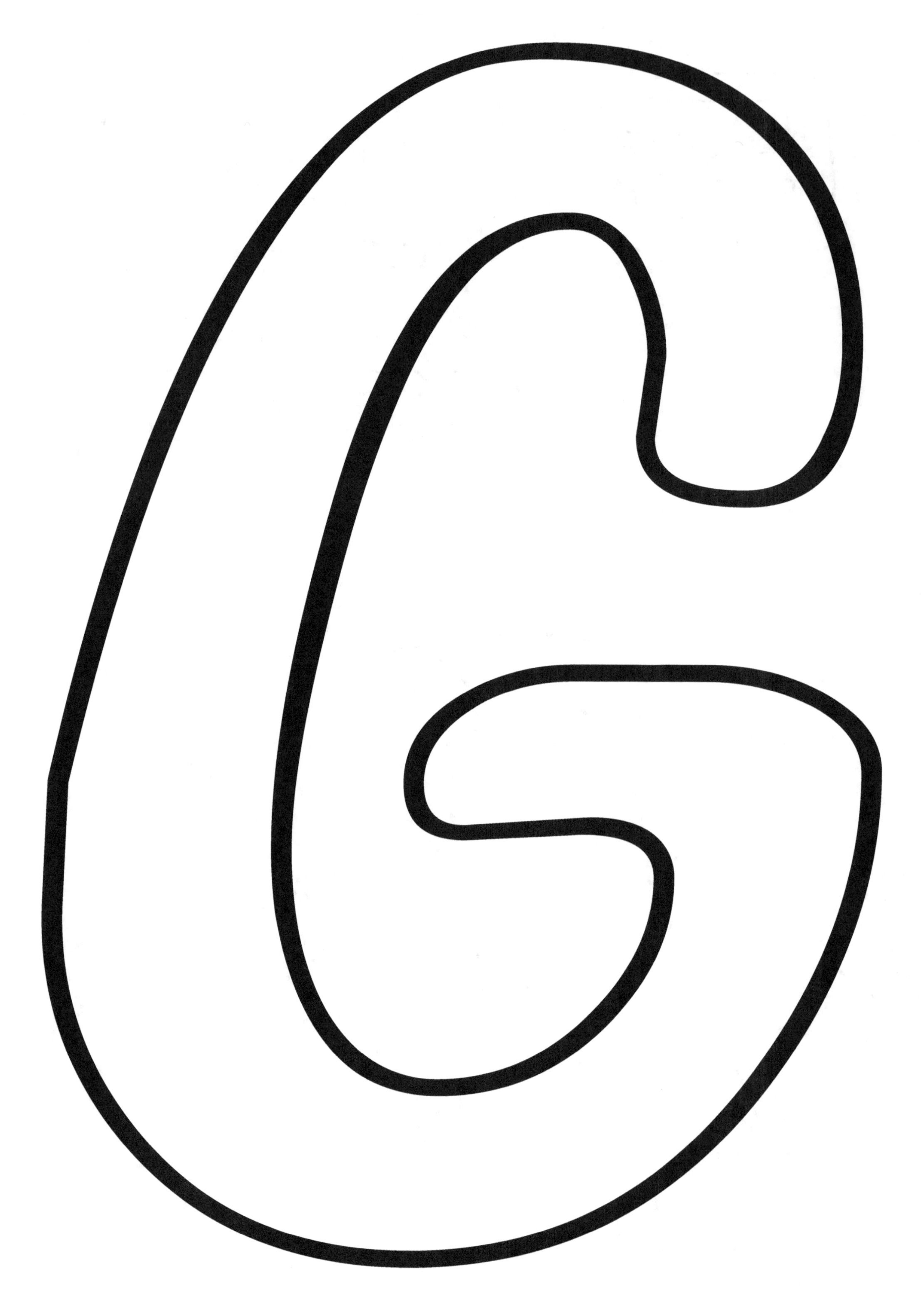

G g is for

Glasses

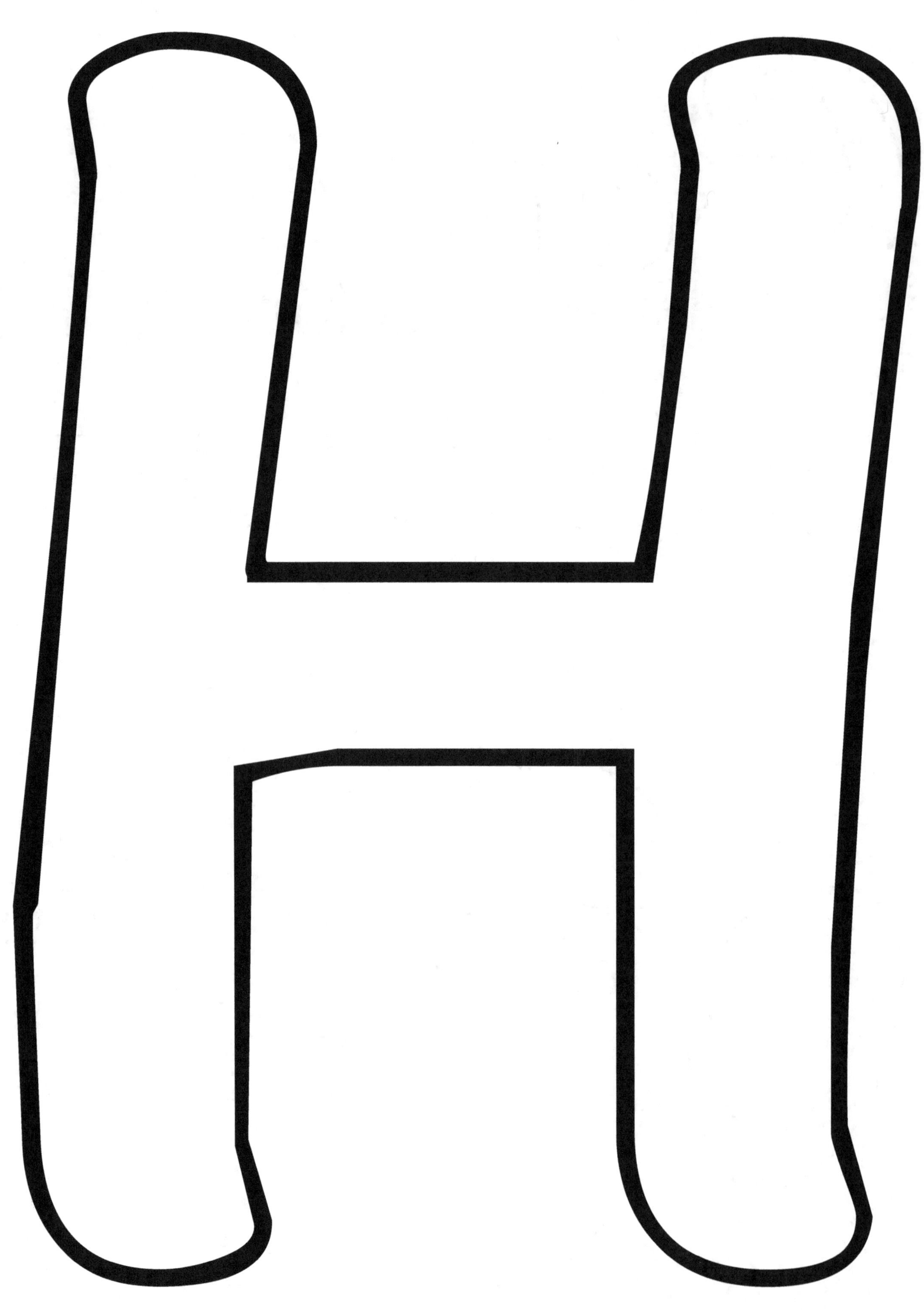

H h

is for

House

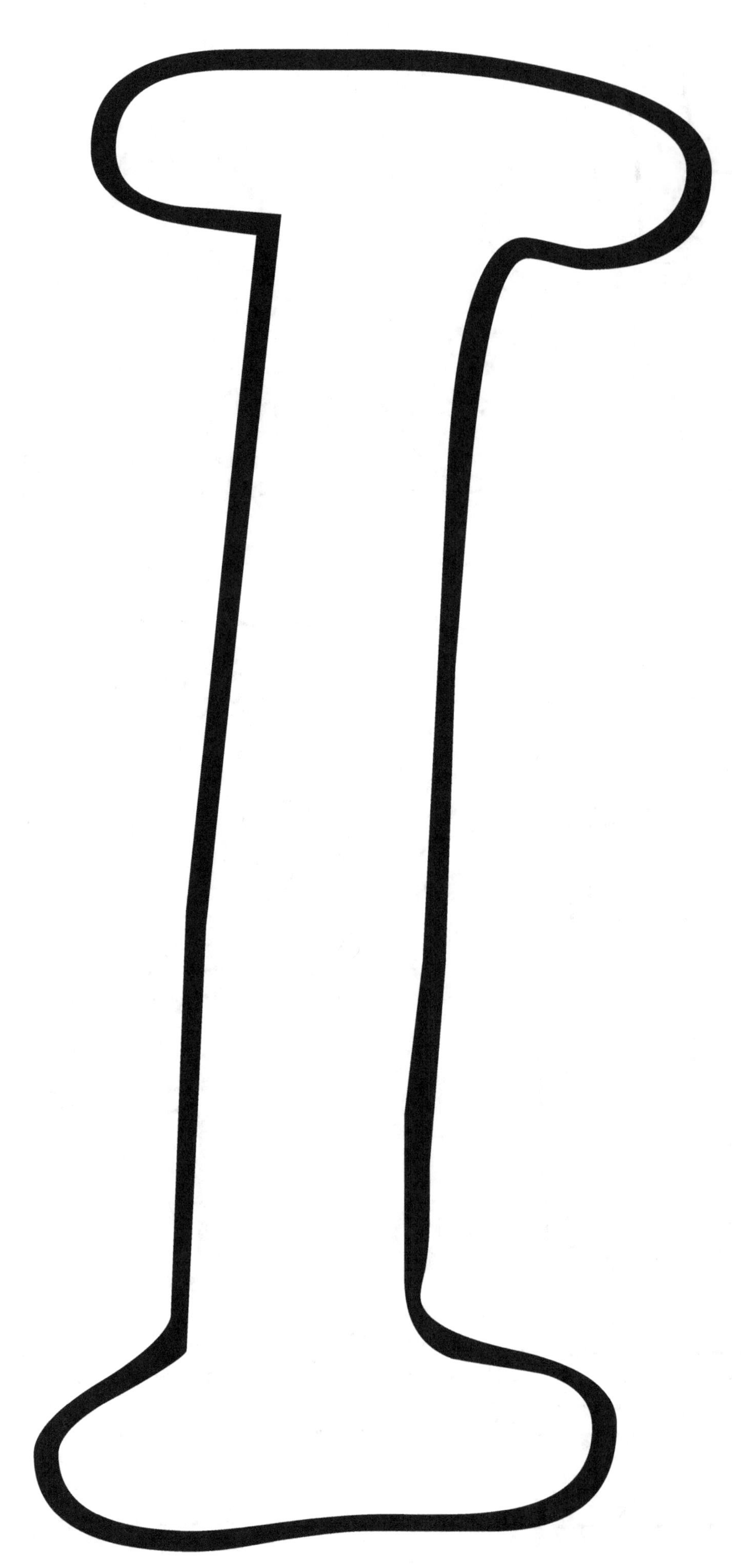

I i

is for

Iron

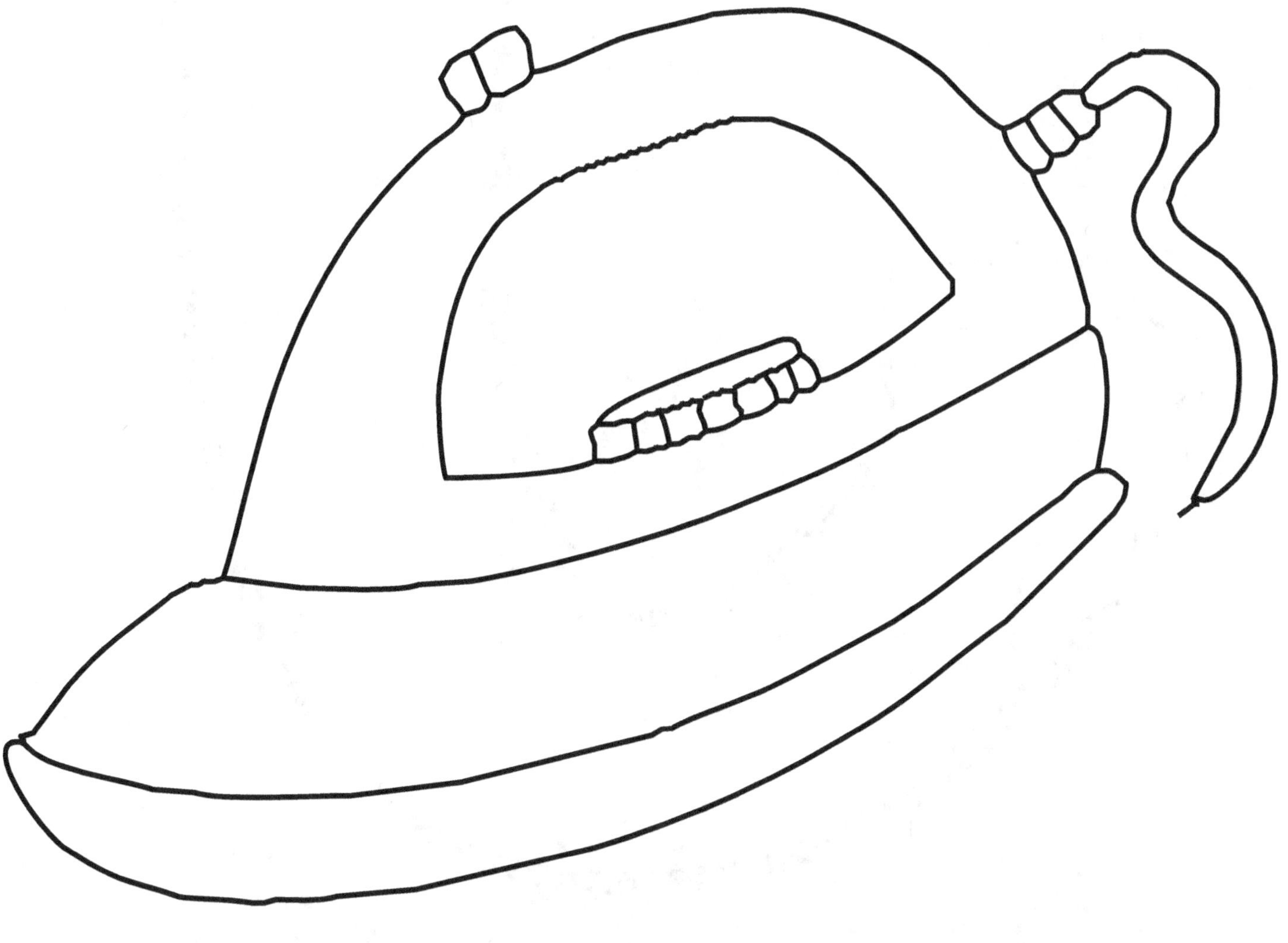

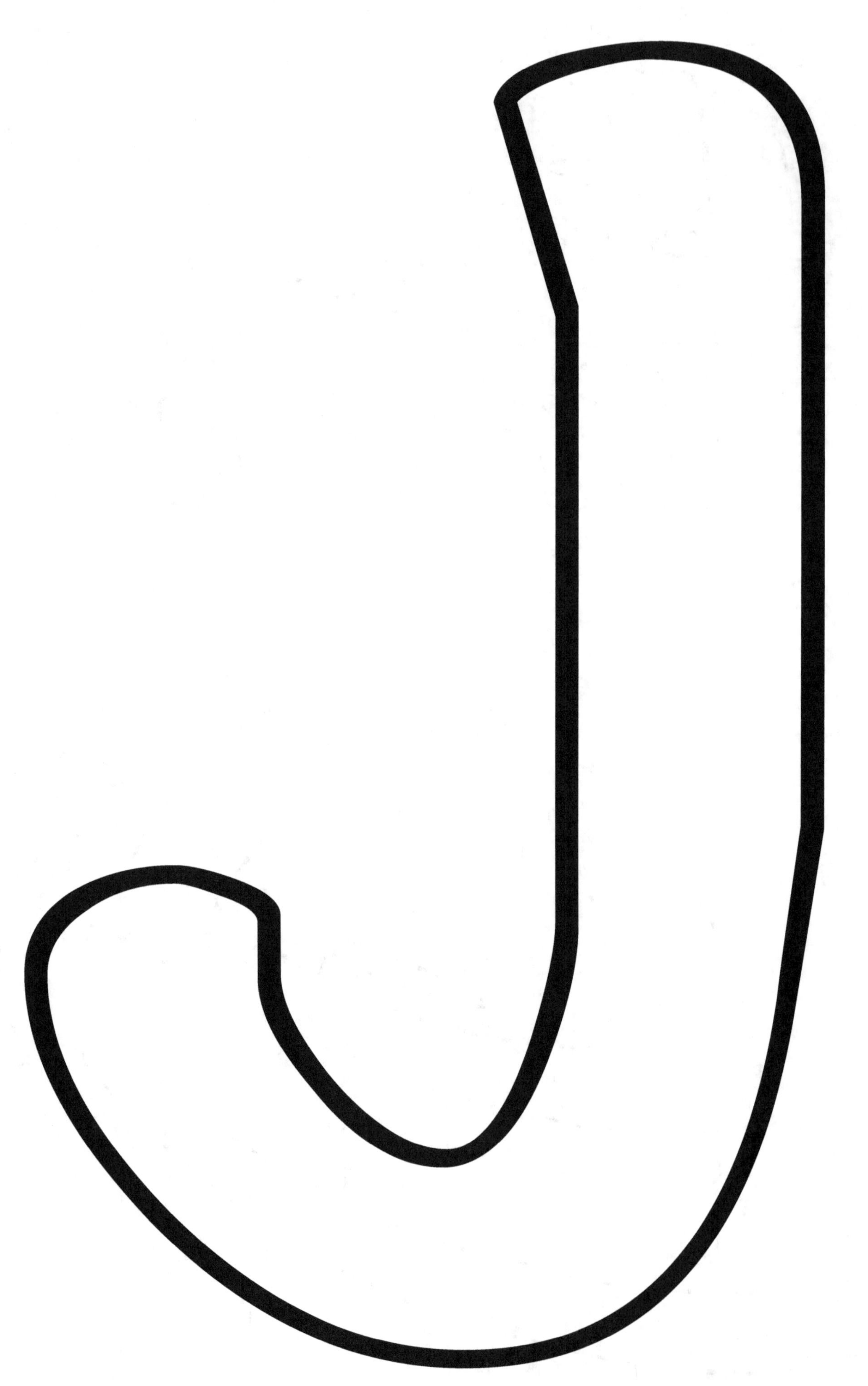

J j is for

Juice

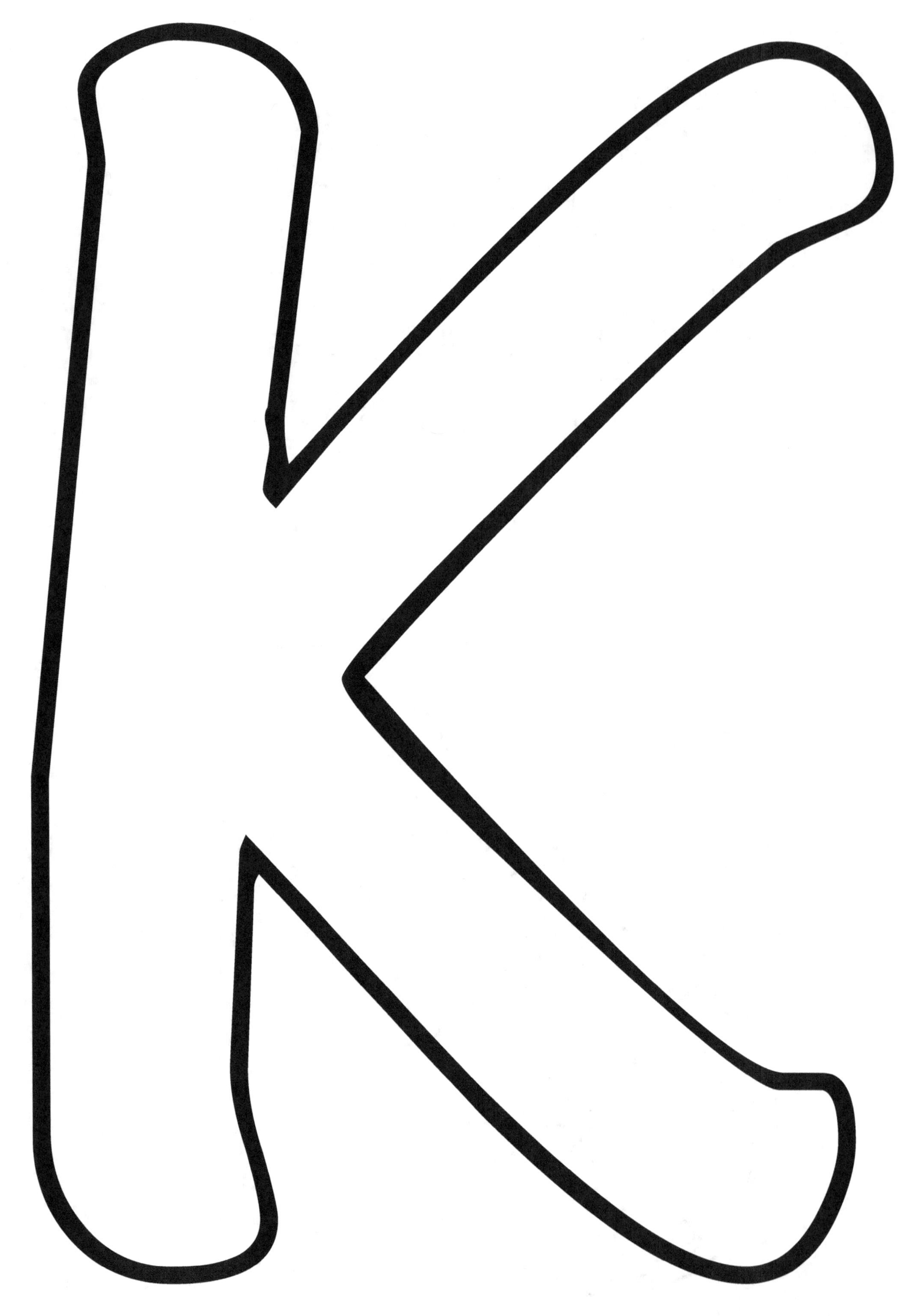

Kk is for
Ketle

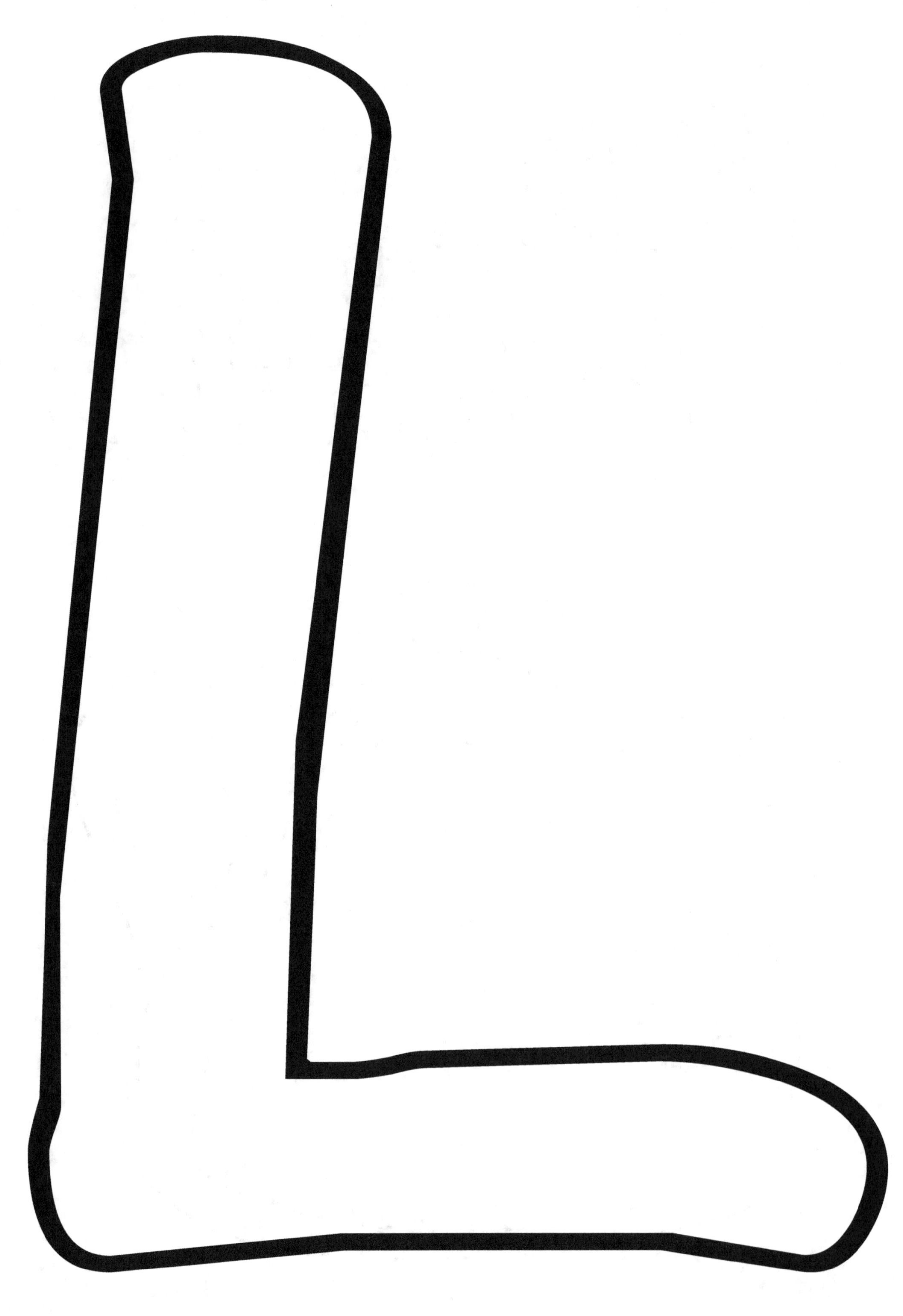

Ll

is for

Lemon

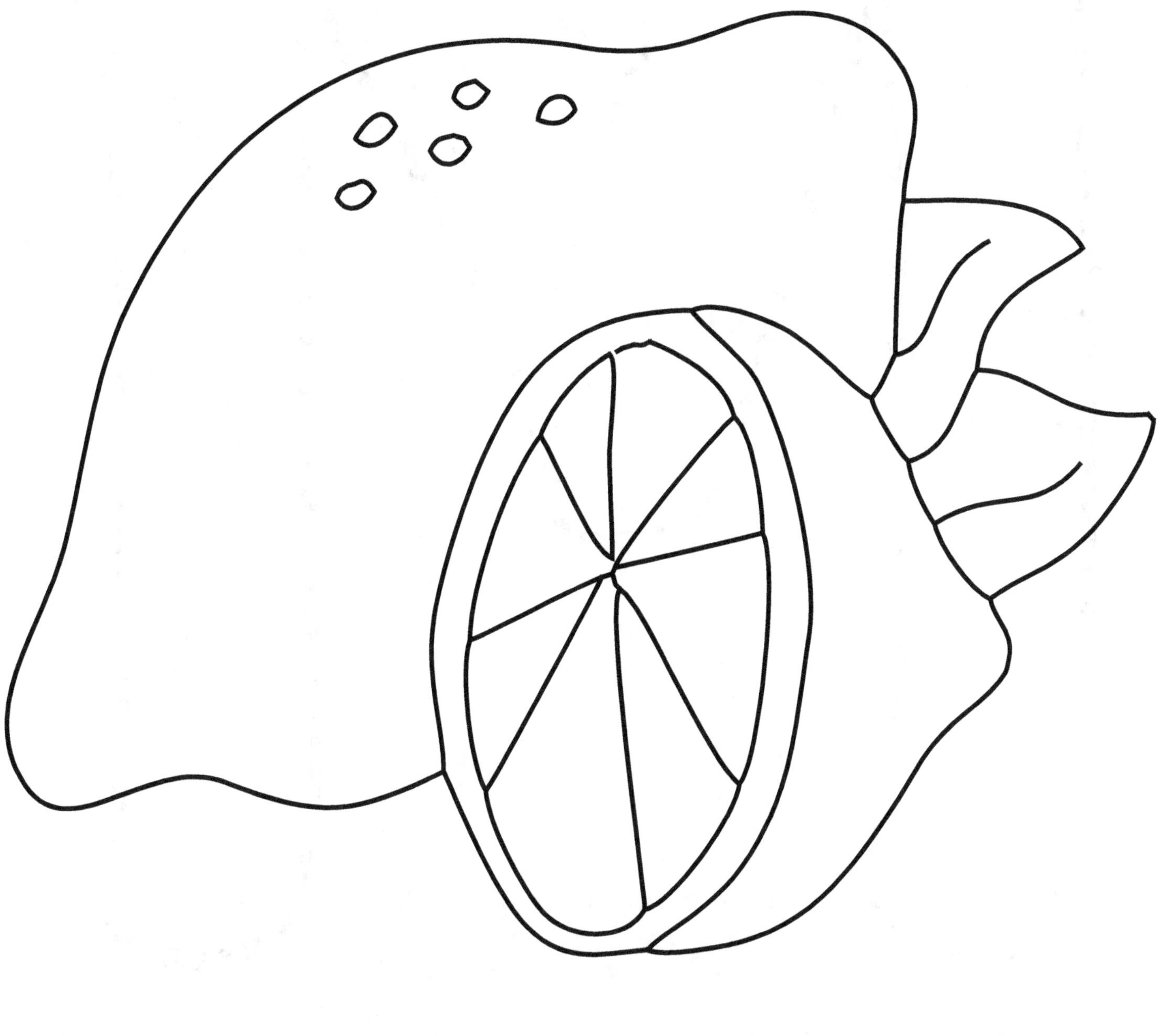

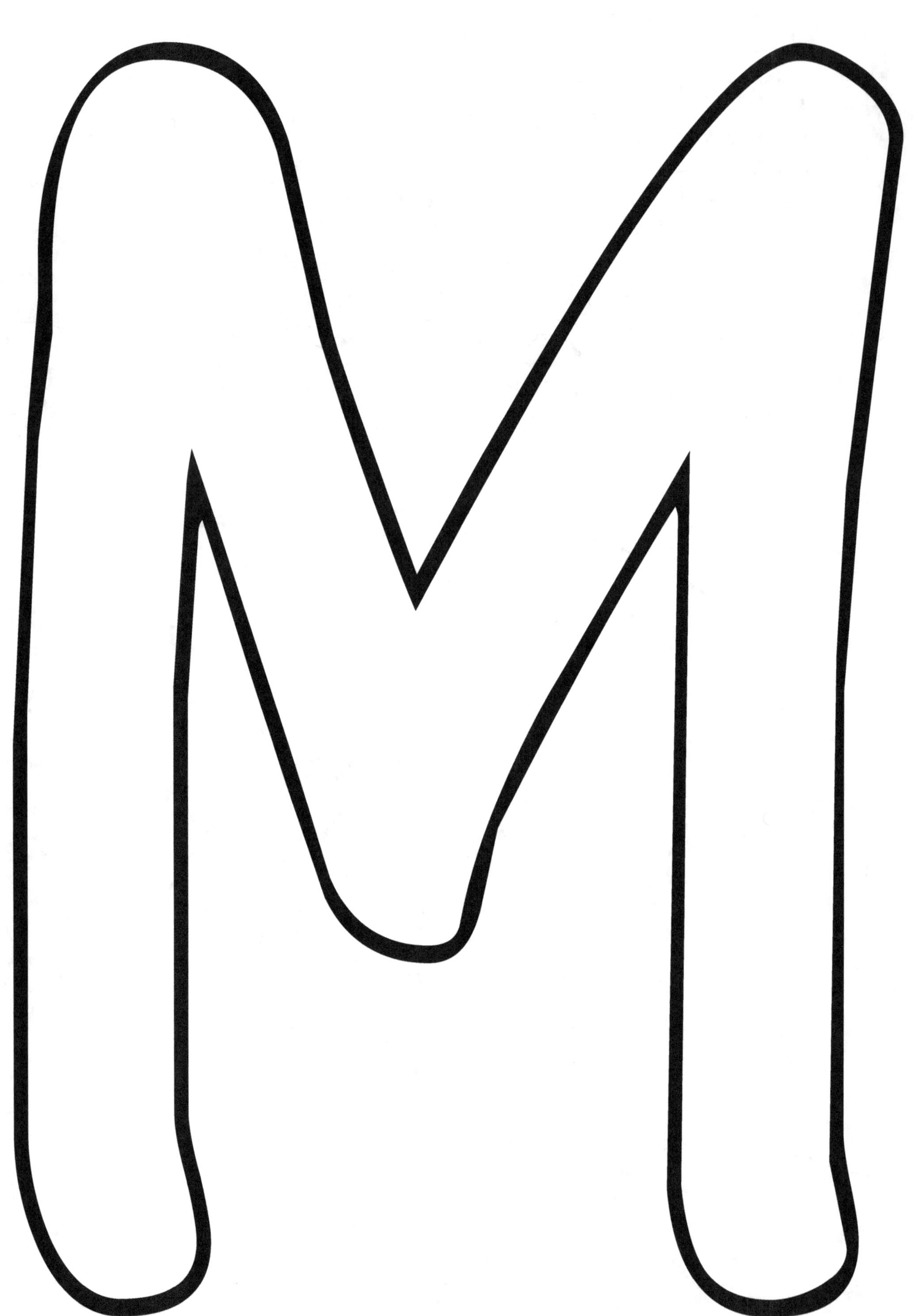

Mm

is for

Mushroom

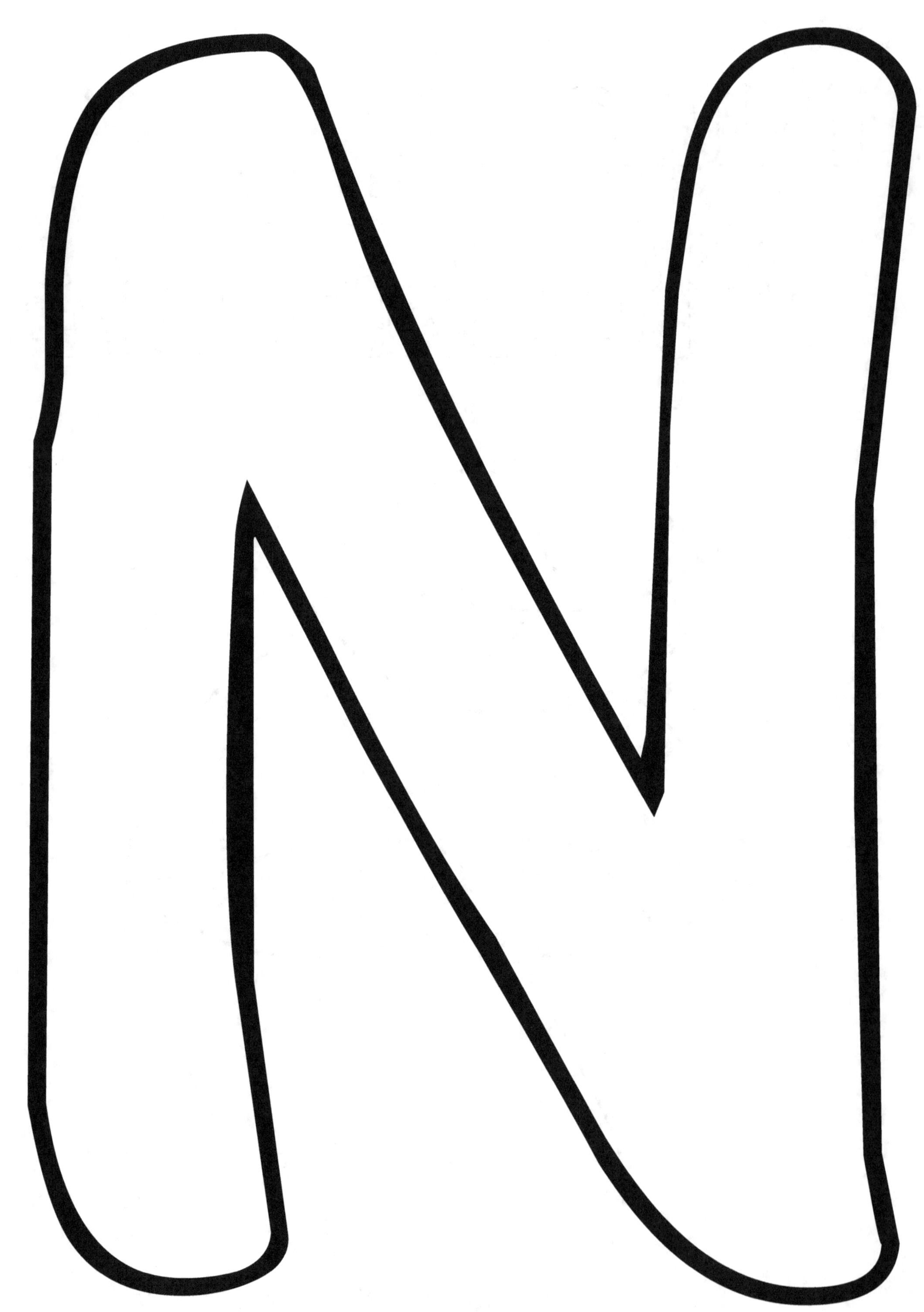

Nn

is for

Nut

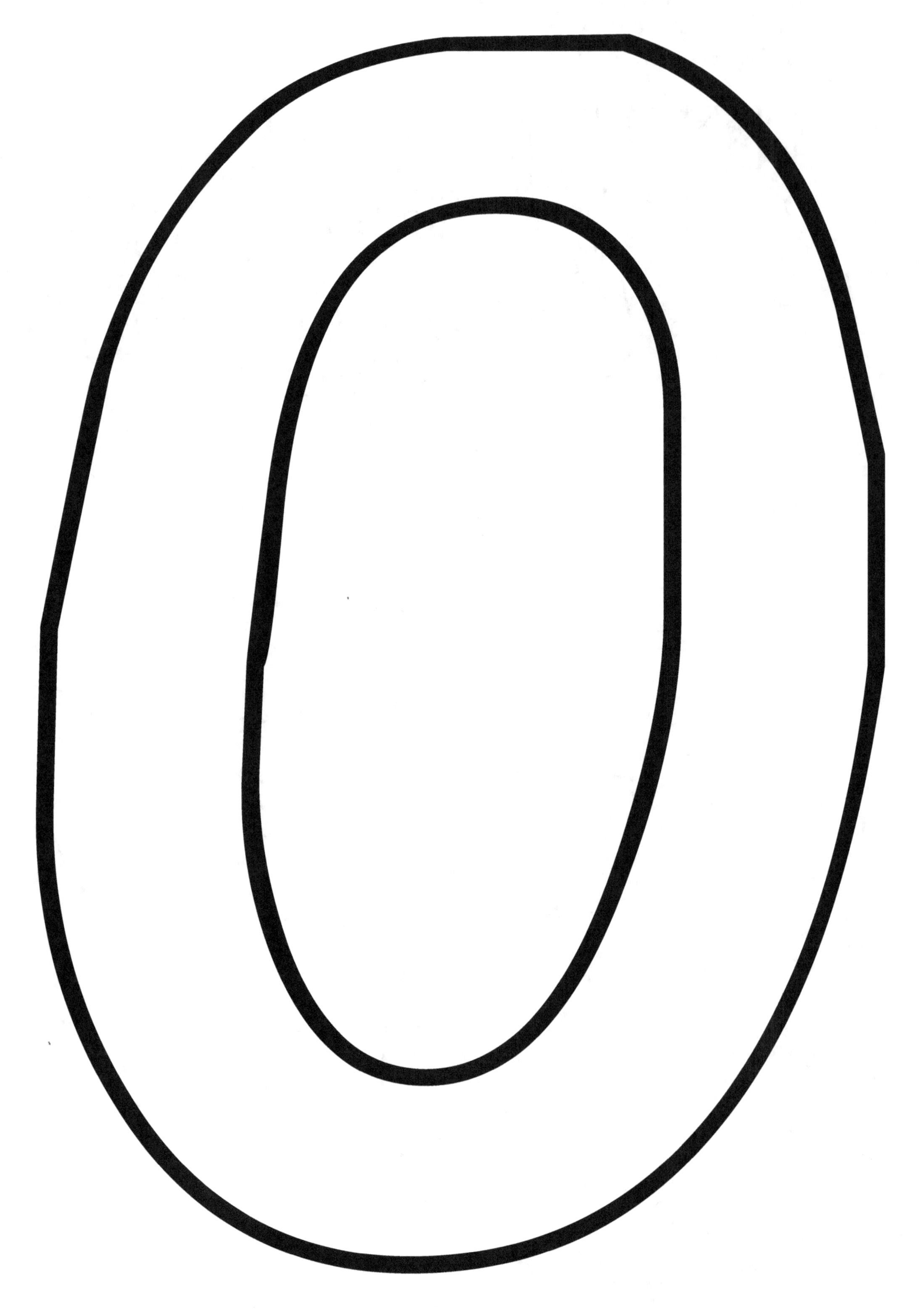

O o
is for
Orange

P p   is for
Pumpkin

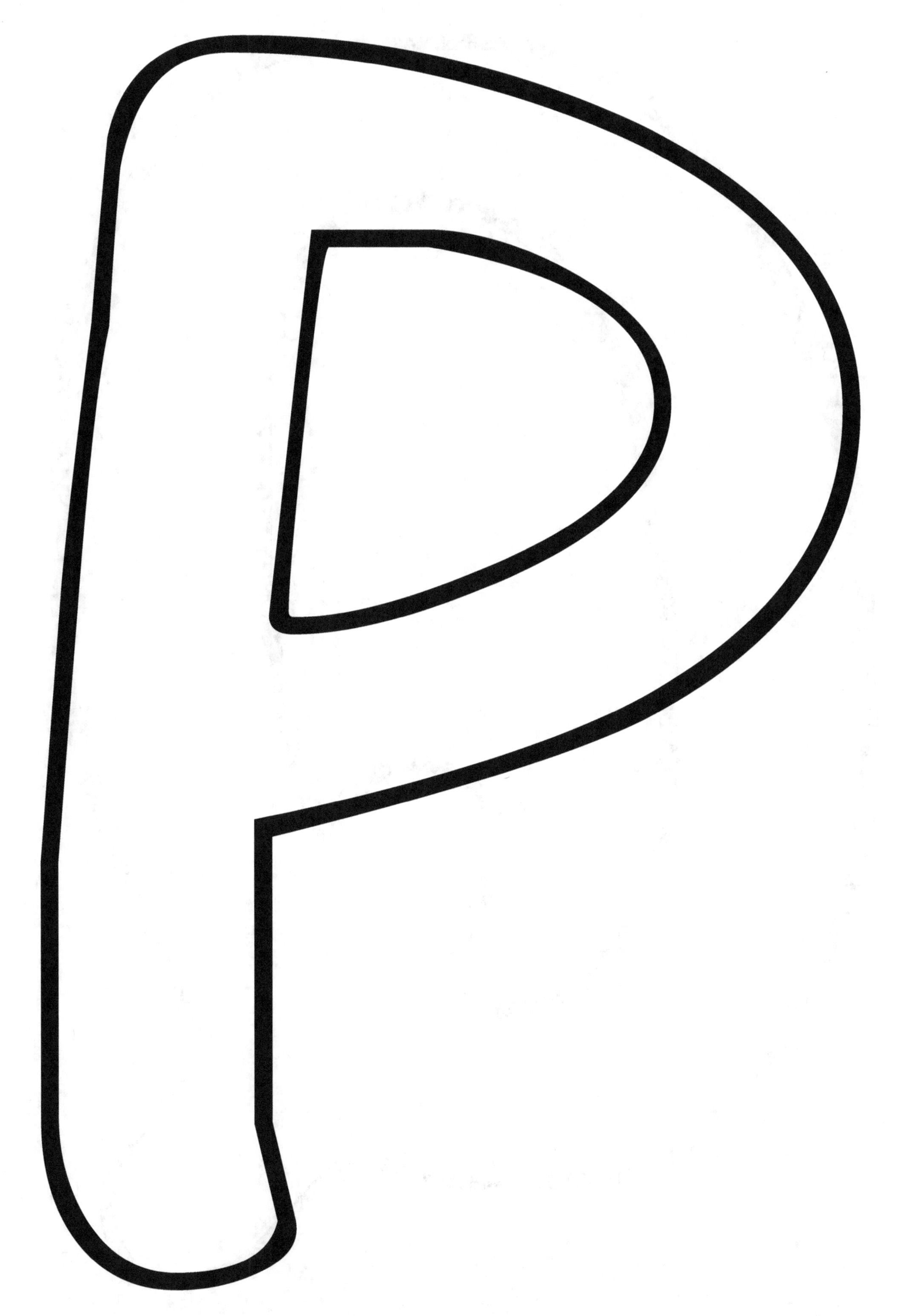

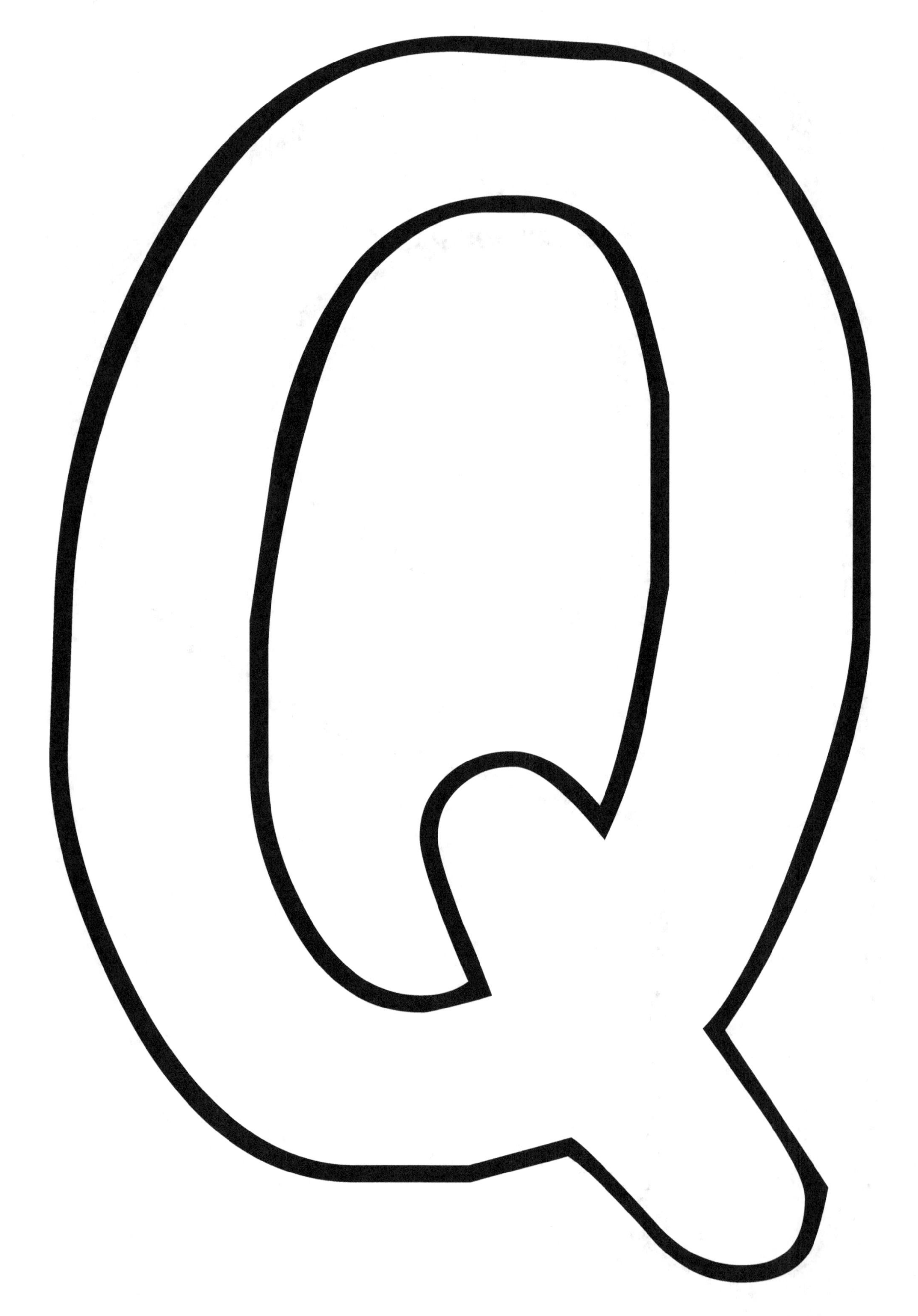

Qq is for
Quill
QUILL

Rr is for

Rain

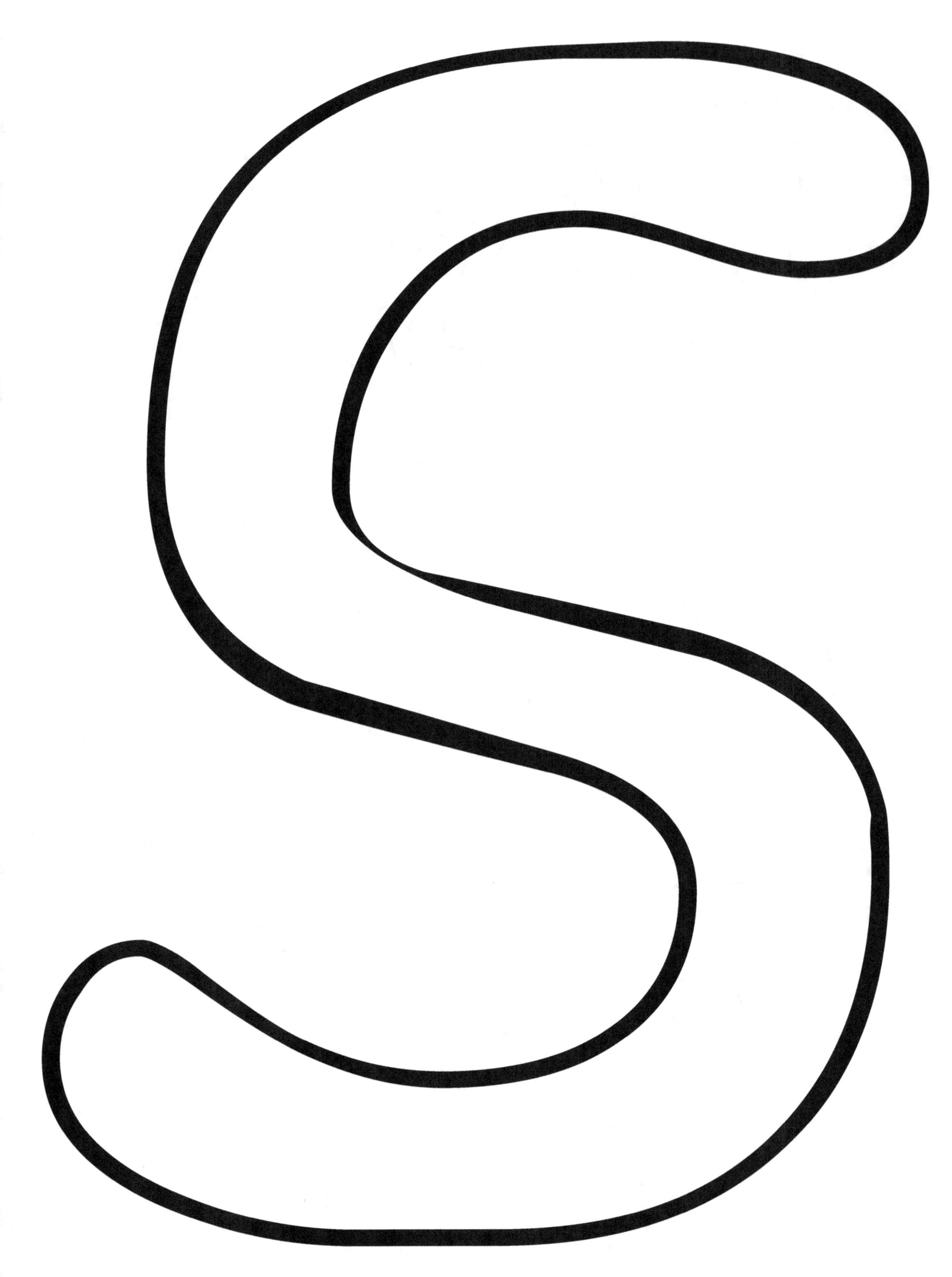

Ss

is for

Shark

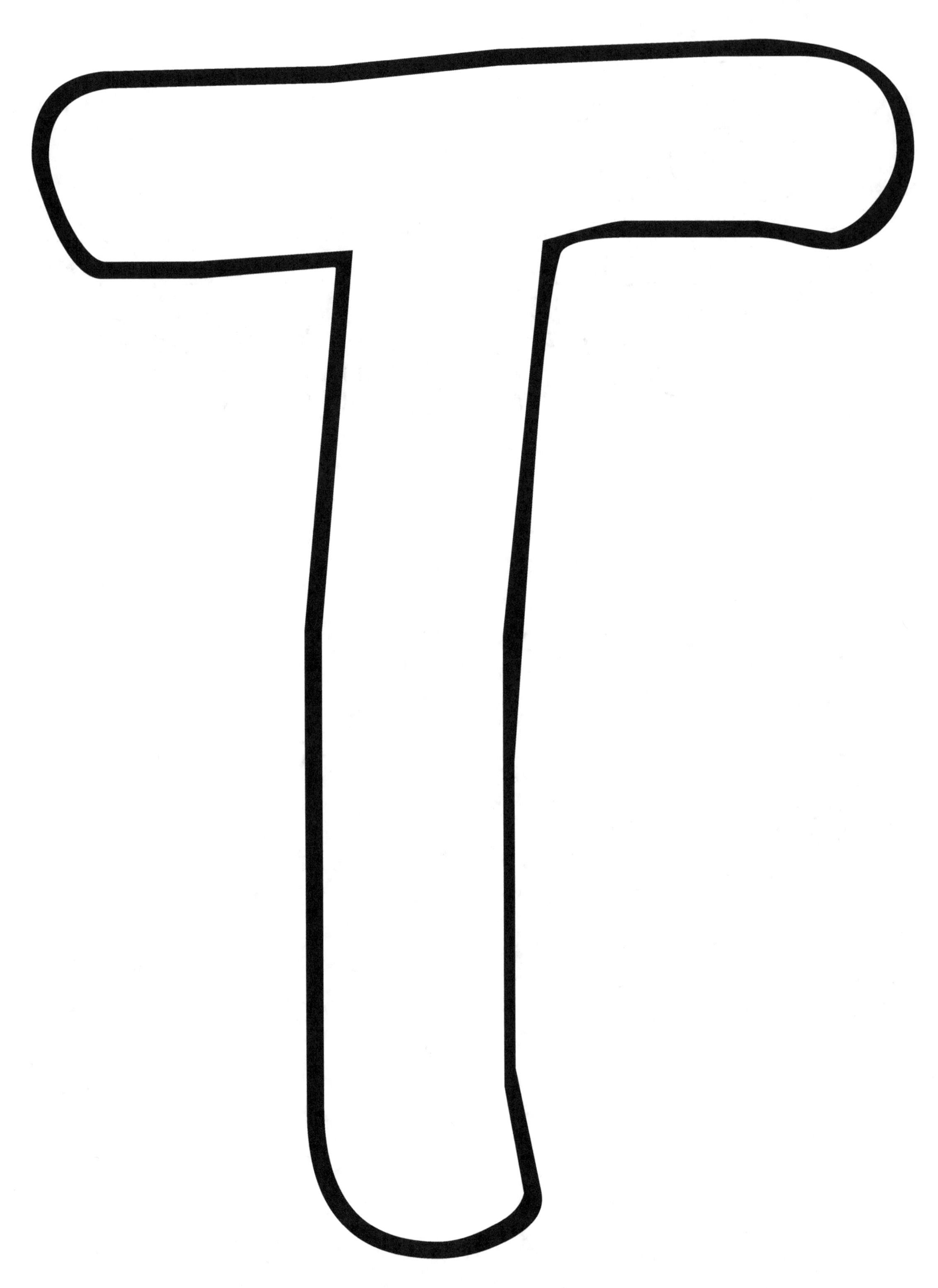

Tt is for Towel

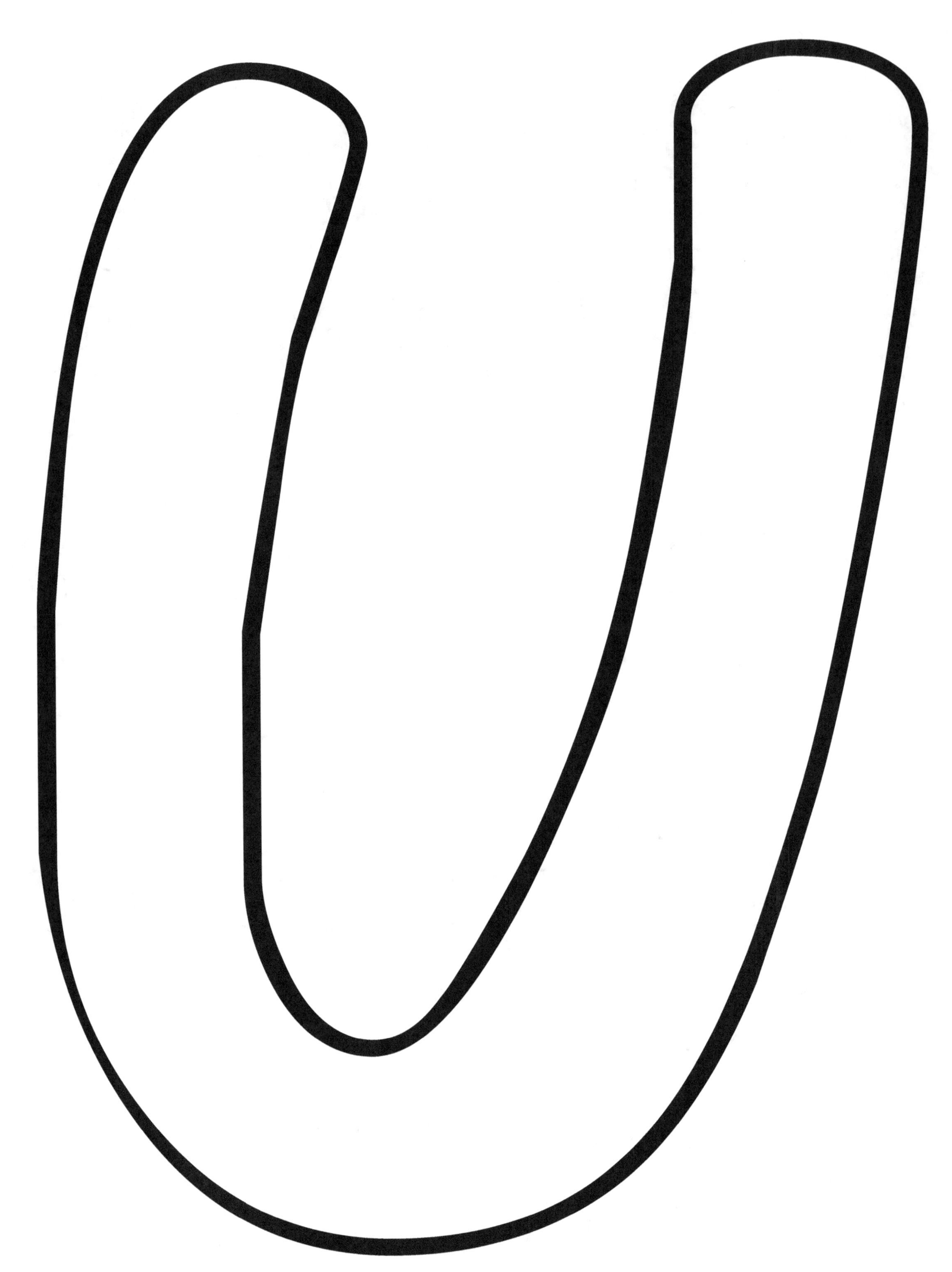

Uu is for Umbrela

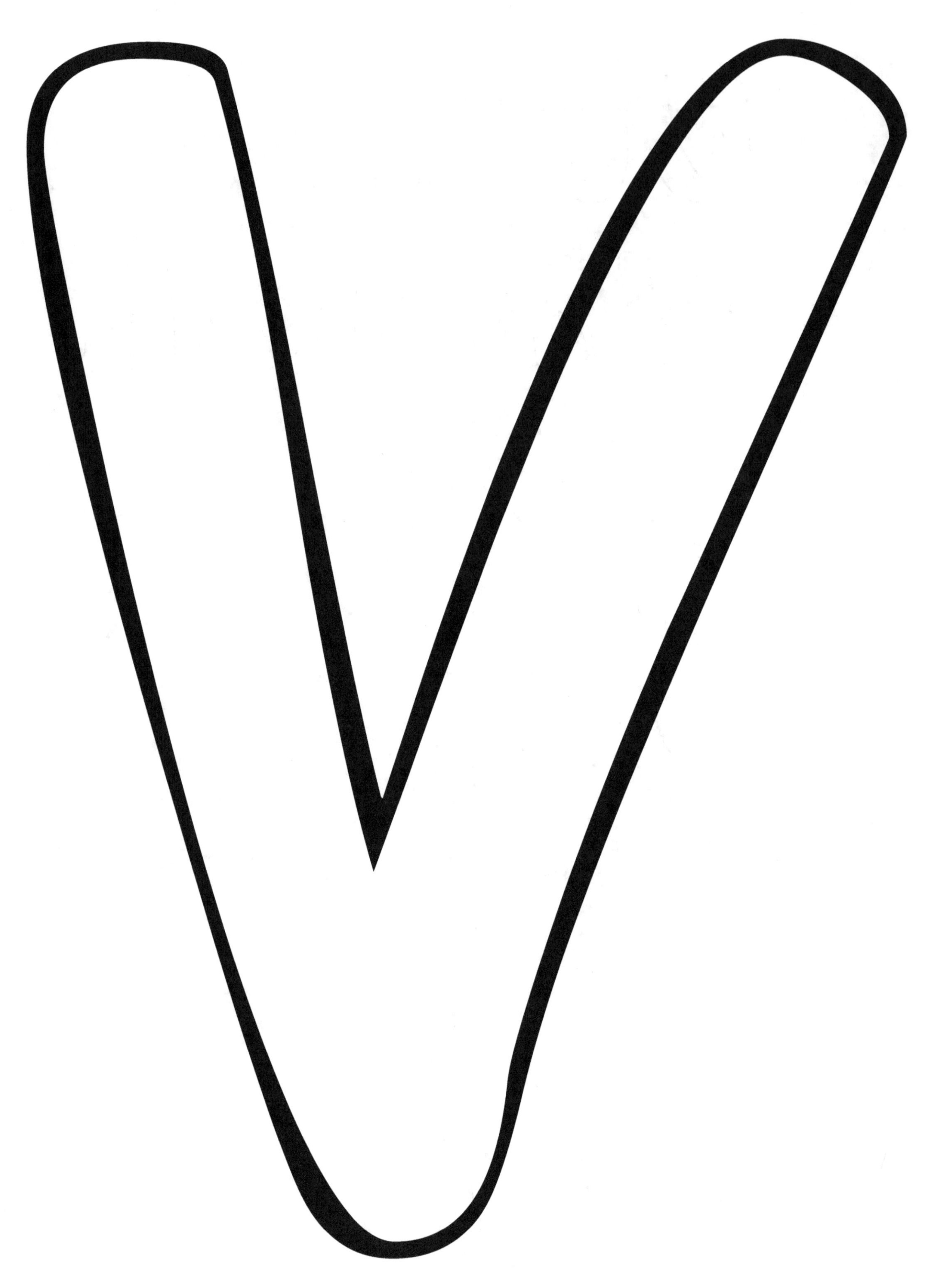

Vv
is for
Vial

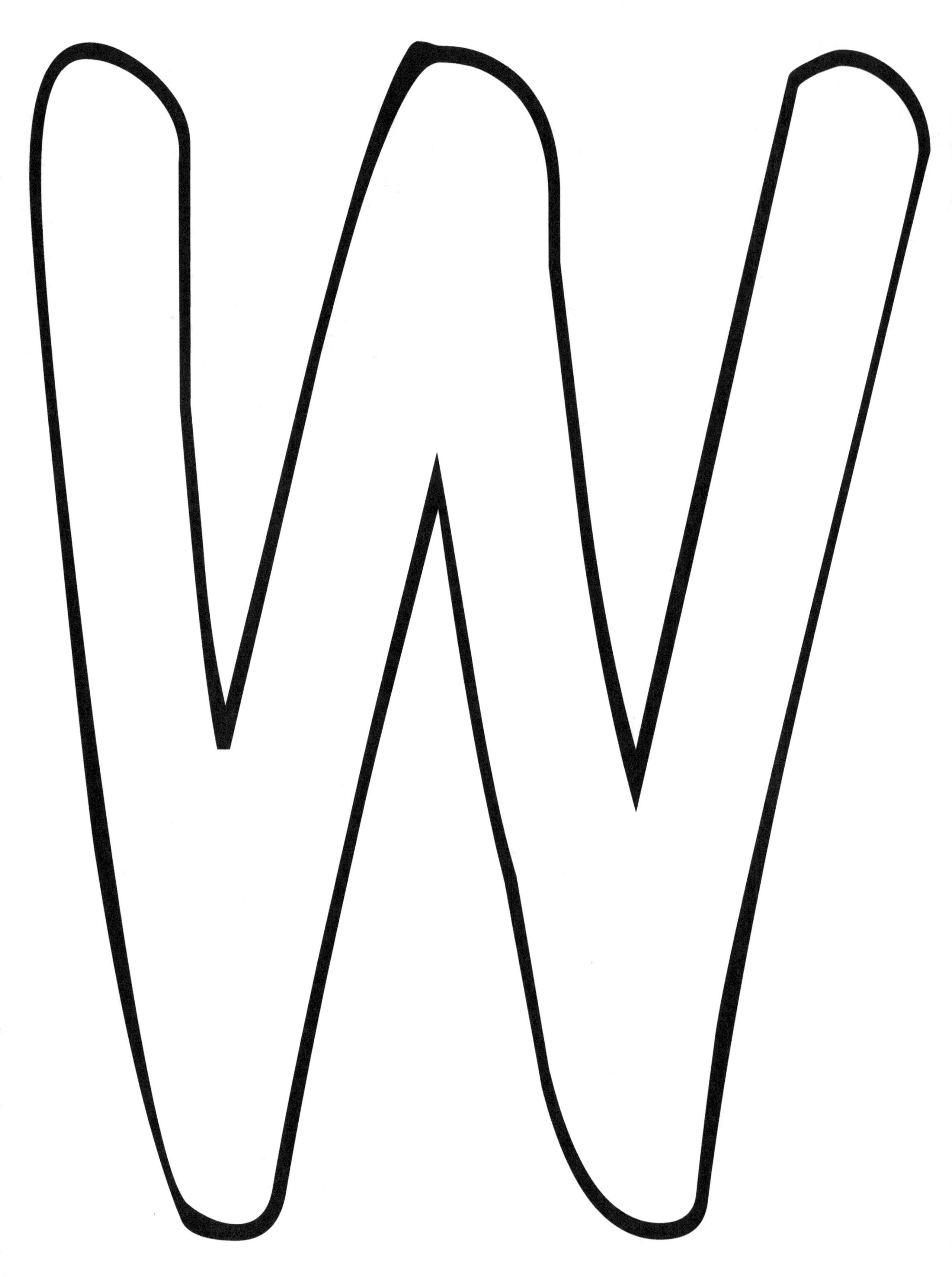

W w is for Window

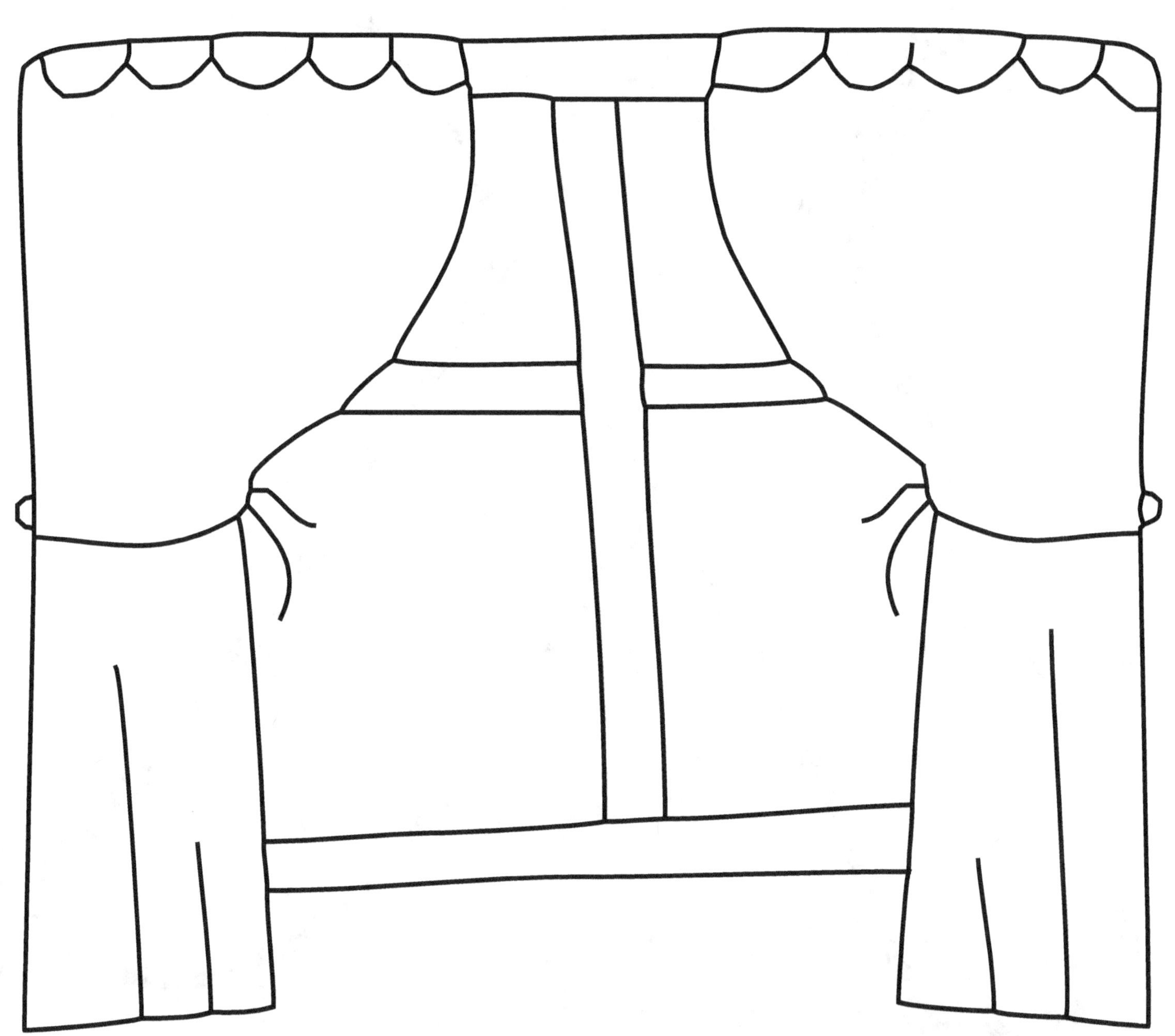

Xx is for Xylophone

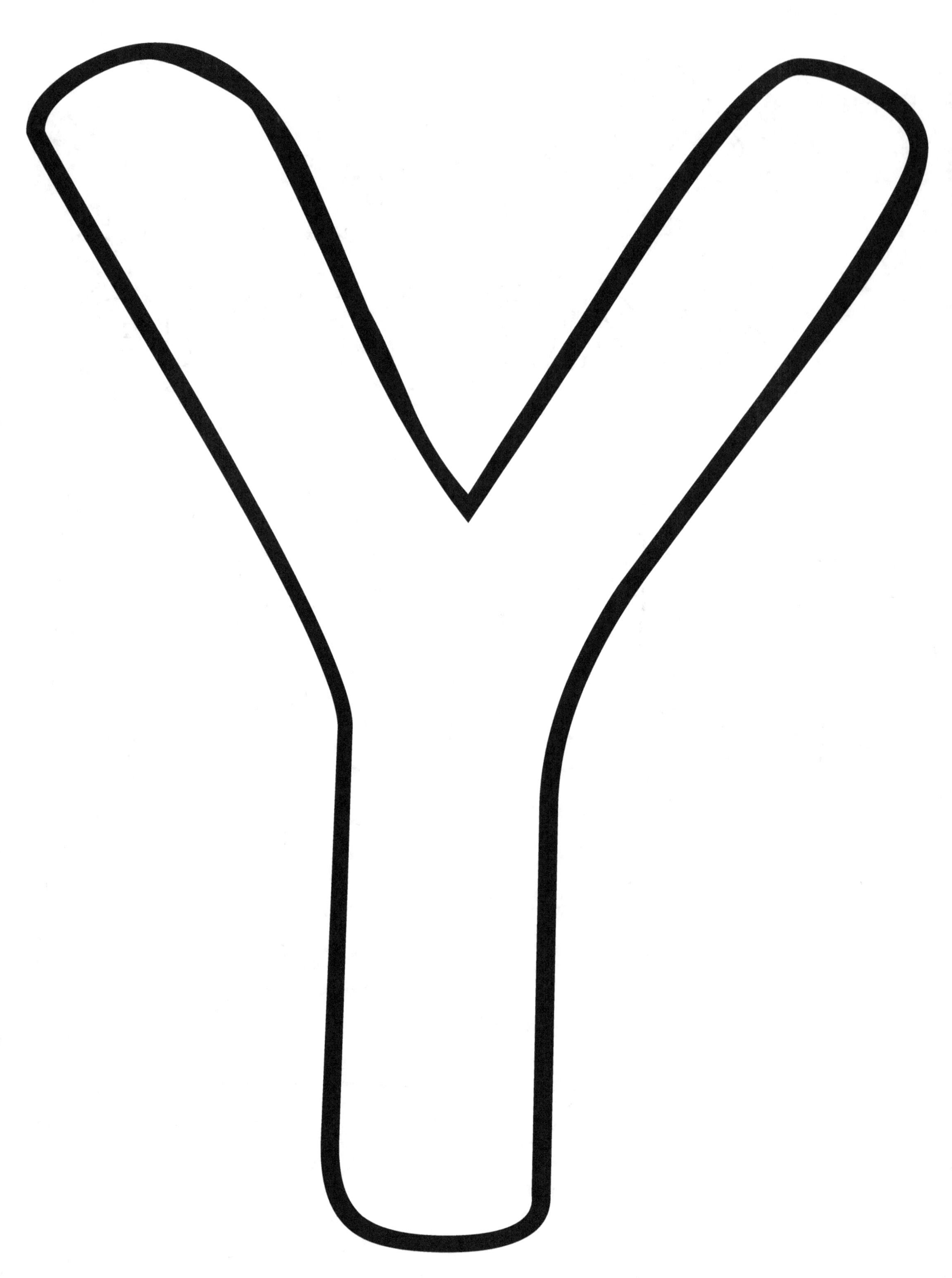

Yy is for
Yogurt

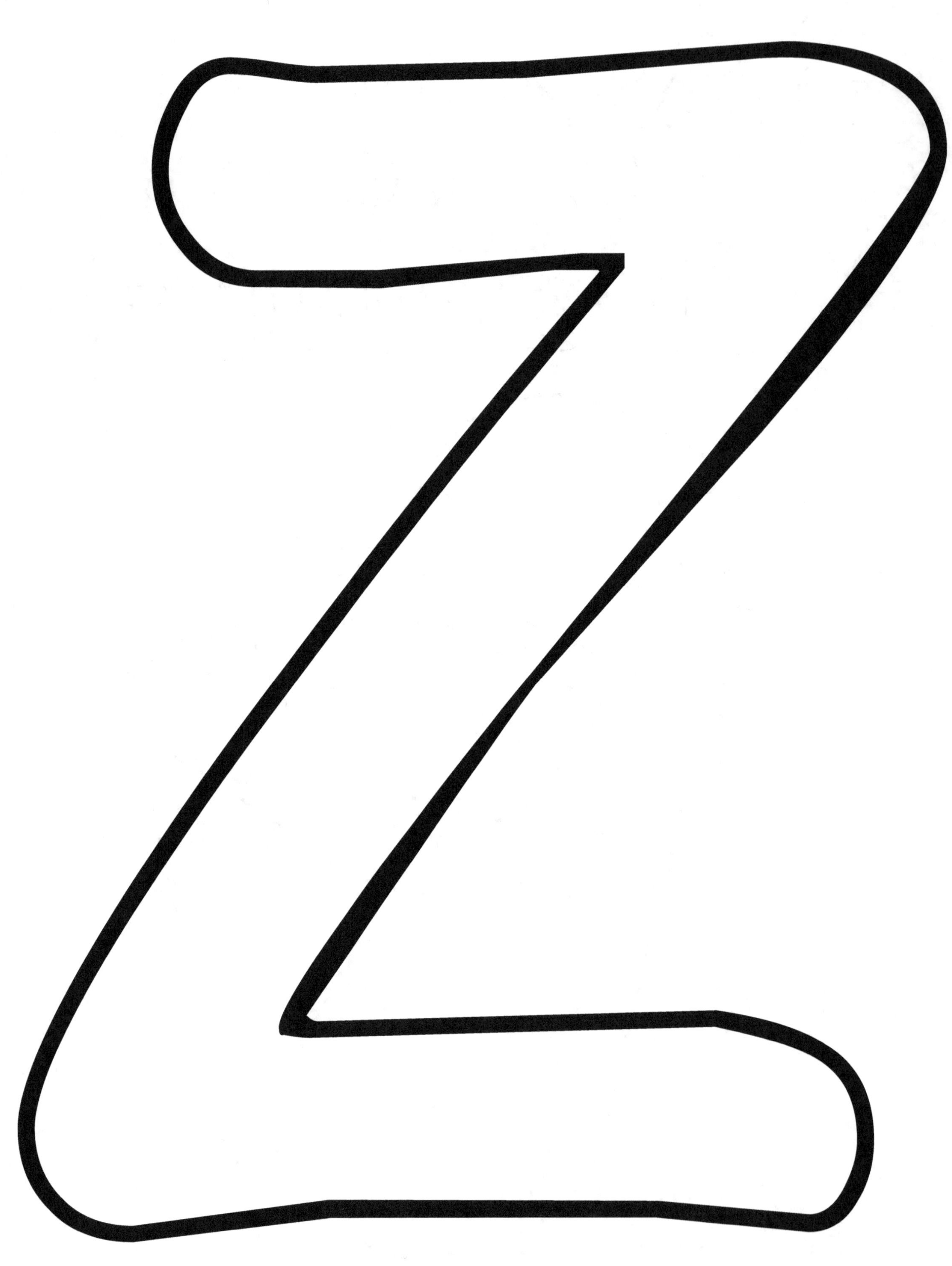

Z z is for
Zebra